CHILDREN LIKE US
Clothes
AROUND THE WORLD

Moira Butterfield

Cavendish
Square

New York

Published in 2016 by Cavendish Square Publishing, LLC
243 5th Avenue, Suite 136, New York, NY 10016

Copyright © 2016 Wayland / Cavendish Square Publishing, LLC

First Edition

Website: cavendishsq.com

This publication represents the opinions and views of the author based on his or her personal experience, knowledge, and research. The information in this book serves as a general guide only. The author and publisher have used their best efforts in preparing this book and disclaim liability rising directly or indirectly from the use and application of this book.

CPSIA Compliance Information: Batch #CW16CSQ

All websites were available and accurate when this book was sent to press. However, it is possible that contents or addresses may have changed since the publication of this book. No responsibility for any such changes can be accepted by either the author or the Publisher.

Cataloging-in-Publication Data

Butterfield, Moira.
Clothes around the world / by Moira Butterfield.
p. cm. — (Children like us)
Includes index.
ISBN 978-1-5026-0836-9 (hardcover) ISBN 978-1-5026-0834-5 (paperback) ISBN 978-1-5026-0837-6 (ebook)
1. Clothing and dress — Juvenile literature. I. Butterfield, Moira, 1960-. II. Title.
GT518.B88 2016
391—d23

Editor: Izzi Howell
Designer: Clare Nicholas
Picture researcher: Izzi Howell
Wayland editor: Annabel Stones

Picture credits:
The author and publisher would like to thank the following for allowing their pictures to be reproduced in this publication: cover Perfect Lazybones/Shutterstock.com; p.3 (t-b) Britta Kasholm-Tengve/iStock, pressdigital/iStock, hbrizard/iStock, lazyllama/Shutterstock; pp.4-5 (c) ekler/Shutterstock, p.4 (t) John de la Bastide/Shutterstock, (b) lazyllama/Shutterstock; p.5 (tl) Maryna Kulchytska/Shutterstock, (tr) Svetlana Arapova/Shutterstock, (b) sansubba/iStock; p.6 (t) hbrizard/iStock, (b) Rolex De La Pena/epa/Corbis; p.7 John de la Bastide/Shutterstock; p.8 Vasily Fedosenko/Reuters/Corbis; p.9 (t) t0zz/Shutterstock, (c) MyImages – Micha/Shutterstock, (b) Wolfgang Kaehler/Corbis; p.10 (tl) Svetlana Arapova/Shutterstock, (cl) Grigorii Pisotsckii/Shutterstock, (br) monkeybusinessimages/iStock; p.11 Danish Ismail/Reuters/Corbis; p.12 Philippe Lissac/Godong/Corbis; p.13 (t) Eric Lafforgue/arabianEye/Corbis, (b) urosr/Shutterstock; p.14 (t) Hugh Sitton/Corbis, (b) Byelikova Oksana/Shutterstock; p.15 Nigel Pavitt/JAI/Corbis; p.16 Chris Hill/National Geographic Creative/Corbis; p.17 (t) Digital Media Pro/Shutterstock, (b) CaronB/iStock; p.18 (tr) Britta Kasholm-Tengve/iStock, (cl) javarman/Shutterstock, (br) lazyllama/Shutterstock; p.19 ML Sinibaldi/Corbis; p.20 pressdigital/iStock; p.21 (t) Zakir Hossain Chowdhury/ZUMA Press/Corbis, (b) Sura Nualpradid/Shutterstock; p.22 (t) nano/iStock, (b) Patrick Seeger/dpa/Corbis; p.23 (t) Craig Lovell/Corbis, (b) vijaya_5712/iStock; p.24 Bartosz Hadyniak/istock; p.25 (t) Tiziana and Gianni Baldizzone/Corbis, (bl) Ursula Alter/iStock, (br) Delpixel/Shutterstock; p.26 (tr) pressdigital/iStock, (cl) Maryna Kulchytska/Shutterstock, (br) salajean/Shutterstock; p.27 Alex Robinson/JAI/Corbis; p.28 (tl) Nigel Pavitt/JAI/Corbis, (cl) veleknez/Shutterstock, (br) Migel/Shutterstock; p.29 sansubba/iStock; p.30 (l-r, t-b) urosr/Shutterstock, ellenamani/iStock, hbrizard/iStock, czekma13/iStock, PerseoMedusa/Shutterstock, vijaya_5712/iStock, John de la Bastide/Shutterstock, angelo lano/Shutterstock, Delpixel/Shutterstock, lifehouseimage/iStock, pressdigital/iStock, Svetlana Arapova/Shutterstock, Abenaa/iStock, Sura Nualpradid/Shutterstock; p.31 (l) pressdigital/iStock, (r) javarman/Shutterstock.

Design elements used throughout: James Weston/Shutterstock, Ramona Kaulitzki/Shutterstock, lilac/Shutterstock, Dacian G/Shutterstock, rassco/Shutterstock, katarina_1/Shutterstock, vectorfreak/Shutterstock, ntnt/Shutterstock, lalan/Shutterstock, Studio Barcelona/Shutterstock, Juli Hansen/Shutterstock, fotolotos/Shutterstock, 21/Shutterstock, Anton Lunkov/Shutterstock, Darya Gribovskaya/Shutterstock, Tatiana_Kost/Shutterstock.

Printed in the United States of America

Contents

All Kinds of Clothes

Are you ready to travel the world and find out about the clothes worn by children just like you? You'll see bright colors and patterns, super shoes, and fantastic hats as you discover what people wear and why.

Many countries have their own festivals. Why is this girl from Trinidad dressed as a bird? Find out why on page 7.

People may wear certain colors to send a message. Why is this Brazilian boy wearing green and yellow? Find out on page 18.

The history of clothes differs in every country. Find out the story behind this Ukrainian girl's flower crown on page 26.

Warm clothes are important in cold countries. What do you think this Nenets boy's coat is made from? Find out on page 10.

People like to wear jewelry. Find out about this Limbu girl's gold headdress on page 29.

Take a journey around the world to discover some fantastic clothes worn by children just like you!

Dress for a Festival

Every country has its own festivals. People often wear special clothes for these parties. This Mexican girl is dressed for the *Día de los Muertos*. This means the "Day of the Dead." For this festival, people dress up as spirits to honor the dead.

This girl is dressed as a skeleton in party clothes.

These children are dressed as flowers. They wear the costumes for the Caracol Festival in the Philippines. At the festival, everybody dresses as animals or plants. They celebrate nature and remind us to protect it.

Everyone hopes to win the prize for the best costume at the festival.

In spring, many Catholic countries hold a big carnival called Mardi Gras. This party marks the start of Lent, a religious time of year. In the past, people wore masks at Mardi Gras to hide who they were. That way, rich and poor people could party together. Today, people wear masks to have fun!

This girl is from Trinidad. She dressed as a bird in a Children's Carnival to celebrate Mardi Gras.

National Costume

At national festivals, people often wear traditional clothes. These are clothes associated with their country. These children are wearing the national dress of Belarus. They wear white or red pants or skirts. They also wear white embroidered shirts.

The embroidery on this clothing is important. It is said to protect the wearer from bad spirits.

In South Korea, the *hanbok* is a traditional outfit. Men and women wear them at festivals and weddings. On top is a short shirt called a *jeogori*. On the bottom, men wear loose pants and women wear long skirts.

The long skirt in a *hanbok* is called a *chima*.

This piper is wearing a tartan kilt. Scottish family groups, called clans, have their own tartan colors and patterns to wear.

The Scottish national outfit includes a fur purse, called a sporran.

This girl is wearing the national costume of Tonga. Her dress is made from woven leaves. Her necklace is made of shells. Her headdress is made from feathers.

The Tongan national costume is made from only natural materials.

Clothes in the Snow

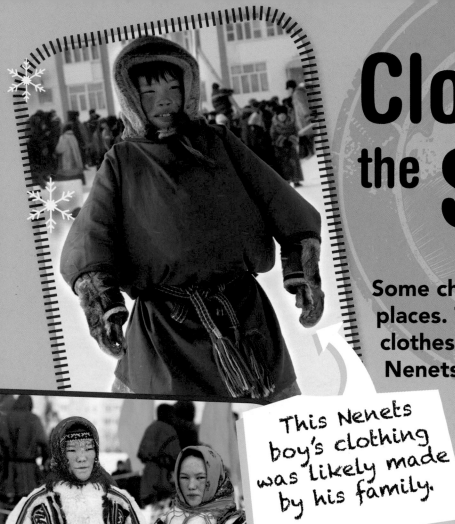

This Nenets boy's clothing was likely made by his family.

Nenets women wear coats made from eight layers of reindeer skin.

Some children live in very cold places. They need to wear warm clothes. This boy belongs to the Nenets people. He lives in Siberia, in Russia. It can reach -58°F (-50°C) there. That's cold! His clothing made from reindeer skin will keep him warm.

Do you see the yellow lenses on these snow goggles? This color cuts down on the glare of the sun.

In the past, everyone wore animal-skin clothing in cold places. Today, people wear special clothing, like this boy's ski jacket. Air gets trapped between the layers of the jacket. This keeps him warmer than animal skins could.

This girl lives in India. She is keeping her feet warm with a kangri. A kangri is a small pot filled with hot embers inside a wicker basket. She wears woolly robes over her clothes. People carry kangri under their robes in winter.

A kangri is like a hot water bottle!

Clothes in the Sun

Some people live in hot places, such as deserts. People in North Africa know they need to wear cooling clothes. Long flowing robes let air move around. They also keep the body safe from the sun.

North African people tend to wear long, loose robes.

In the desert, wind can bring sandstorms. Plus, the sun can burn skin. That's why people in the Middle East often wear a special scarf. They wrap it around their faces. It keeps them safe when it's hot or windy.

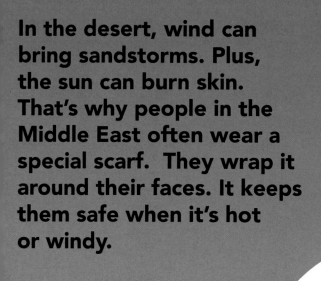

The scarf Middle Eastern people wear is called a kaffiyeh.

This African girl belongs to the Namibian Himba tribe. Himba women and children cover their skin, clothes, and hair with ground-up red rock and butter. This paste acts as a sunscreen. It also keeps bugs away.

The Himba use the red paste to coat their hair.

Clothes in the Rain Forest

Some people live deep in the rain forest. They make their clothes from plants and animal skins. Children in the Amazon rain forest in South America often wear skirts made from dried plant parts. Their clothes help to keep them cool.

The Amazon people add beads made of wood or seeds to their clothes.

This woman is from Papua New Guinea. Her headdress is made from bird feathers.

In countries where it's very hot, people do not wear a lot of clothing. Jewelry and face paint are often worn instead. Here, people wear their best jewelry and headdresses to impress other people.

Rain forests have a lot of plants. People use the plants to make clothing, jewelry, and other things. This woman lives in Ethiopia, Africa. Her umbrella is made from the dried leaves of the "false banana" plant that grows around her home.

The green plants here are "false banana" plants. They were used to make the umbrella.

Dress for Dancing

Special dances need special clothes. This Irish girl is dressed for Irish stepdancing. Her dress is covered with designs. They come from a famous Irish book, the Book of Kells. Boys wear black pants or kilts. Sometimes they wear coats with designs like those on the girls' dresses.

In Irish dance, you must keep your hands and body straight. You can move your legs and feet, though.

This boy is dressed to dance a Fancy Dance. This Native American dance is performed to the beat of a drum. His colorful clothing stands for the spirit of the rainbow. Fancy Dancers compete at powwows. Powwows are Native American events held in Canada and the USA.

Fancy Dancers are judged on their costumes, as well as their dancing.

Flamenco is a traditional dance in southern Spain. Girls wear long, frilled dresses. Boys wear tight-fitting pants and short jackets. They stamp their feet as they dance to Spanish guitar music.

Flamenco costumes are eye-catching, just like the dance.

Colorful Clothes

The color of clothes is sometimes important. People of the Masai tribe in Kenya wear red clothing. They believe red is the color of bravery. They also believe it scares away lions. The bright color helps them see each other on the plains, too.

This Masai girl is wearing a beaded neck plate.

Masai robes can be wrapped around the body in many different ways.

People sometimes wear colors that show where they come from. This Brazilian boy is wearing green and yellow. These are two of the colors on Brazil's flag. The national sports teams of Brazil wear yellow and green, too.

The green on Brazil's flag stands for rain forests. The yellow is for gold.

Boys leave their families to become Buddhist monks. They go live in a monastery.

Buddhist monks in India and Tibet wear red or orange robes. It is said that long ago, Buddha Gautama, the founder of Buddhism, chose these colors. At the time, orange and red were the cheapest dyes. He wanted to show everyone that Buddhist monks were humble. They did not have a lot of wealth.

Working Clothes

This paddy hat is made from plant fibers. They are tightly woven to keep out water.

It's important to wear the right clothes for the job. This Asian girl is helping to harvest rice. She is wearing a paddy hat to keep her safe from the sun and the rain. She can scoop water into the hat and use it to cool down, too.

This girl is harvesting water lilies from a lake in Bangladesh. She will also help to sell them at the local market. She will wear the beautiful lily hat she's made.

The water lily is the national flower of Bangladesh.

Carrying-scarves are common in Asia and Africa.

This Ghanaian girl has folded up a thick scarf on her head. She uses it to help her to carry a basket of fruit. It will help her to balance heavy loads as she walks along.

Clothes for Special Days

This Jewish boy is dressed for his bar mitzvah. This is a religious ceremony that takes place when Jewish boys are 13 years old. He is wearing a prayer shawl called a *tallit*. He also wears a traditional head covering called a *kippah*.

A *schäppel* takes a long time to make. All of the beads are sewn on by hand!

After the bar mitzvah, there will be a family party for the boy.

In the Black Forest in Germany, children dress in traditional clothes for their First Communion. This is a Christian ceremony. The girls are wearing hats known as *schäppel*, which are made from ribbons and pearl beads.

In India, everybody dresses up for a wedding. They wear bright clothing with beautiful designs. The bride and the female guests will often get their hands painted with traditional henna patterns. Indian brides wear red for good luck.

Indian wedding guests often wear outfits with embroidered patterns.

Henna is a paste that stains the skin red.

Special Shoes

These colorful shoes are called *juttis*. They are worn all over northern India. Cows are sacred in Hindu India. At festival times they wear their own special *juttis*!

Juttis are a common sight in local markets in northern India.

These reindeer-skin boots are called *skaller*. They are made to keep feet warm and dry in the cold. They've been worn for centuries by the Sami people. The Sami live in the far north of Scandinavia. *Skaller* used to be worn with skis. The curled-up toes helped to stop the skis from slipping off.

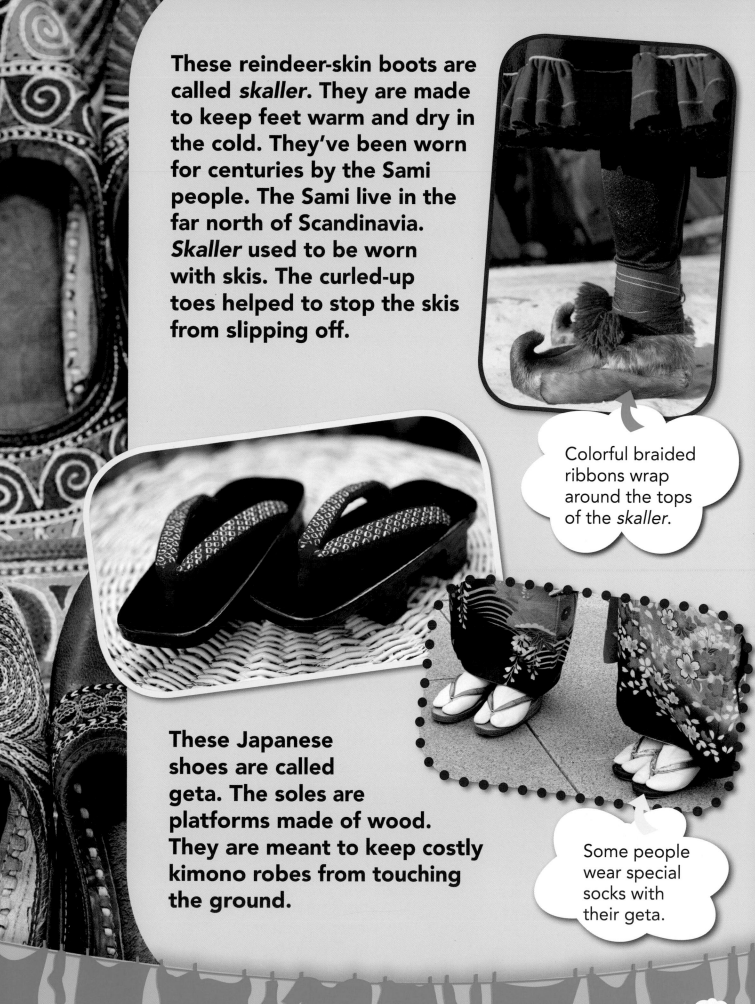

Colorful braided ribbons wrap around the tops of the *skaller*.

These Japanese shoes are called geta. The soles are platforms made of wood. They are meant to keep costly kimono robes from touching the ground.

Some people wear special socks with their geta.

Fantastic Hats

Hats sometimes tell us about the people who wear them. There are many tribes in northern Thailand. Each tribe has its own hat style. This girl is from the Hmong tribe in the far north of Thailand. She is wearing her colorful beaded hat for a New Year festival.

An old Hmong story says evil spirits are scared away by beaded clothing.

In Ukraine, girls and unmarried women wear pretty wreaths of flowers called *vinoks*. In the past, young women used to place their *vinoks* into a river with a candle on top. Young men would jump into the water to catch the *vinok* of the girl they loved.

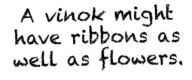

A vinok might have ribbons as well as flowers.

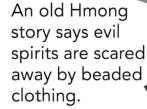

This Romanian boy wears a traditonal hat. The flower is made from small pieces of cloth.

Hats are useful! This boy is wearing a woolly hat called a chullo. He lives in the Andes Mountains of South America. It can be very cold there. His hat helps to keep him warm. It's made from the wool of a local llama.

Andean villages have their own special patterns and colors for chullos.

All Kinds of Jewelry

People around the world like to wear jewelry. In Kenya, girls from the Pokot tribe wear necklaces woven from thick grasses. They also add wooden beads and buttons. In Ethiopia, girls from the Mursi tribe wear large wooden discs in their ears.

This Pokot girl's necklace has been rubbed with animal fat and red rock dust.

Skin stretches around the disc in this Mursi girl's ear.

Women from the Kayan tribe in Burma and Thailand wear metal neck rings. Girls start wearing them at the age of five or six. They can remove the neck rings when they reach 15. Many women choose to leave them on.

The neck ring is one metal coil that wraps around the neck many times.

This gold headdress is called a *sesephung*. It has a moon made of red coral.

This girl is one of the Limbu people. They live in eastern Nepal and Tibet. Limbu women are known for their jewelry. It is made from gold, silver, coral, and glass. The jewelry is meant to look like things in nature, such as the sun or flower buds.

Art Station

Here are some ideas for getting creative and designing your own world!

- Design a new national costume for your country. You could use the colors of the flag.

- Design an outfit for someone living in a really cold, icy place. Label your outfit with your ideas for keeping warm.

- Design an outfit for someone living in a hot location, perhaps a rain forest or a desert. Label your outfit with your ideas for keeping cool and safe in the sun.

- Design a crazy, amazing pair of shoes or a hat. Who would wear them?

Glossary

Buddhism A religion that follows the teachings of Buddha.

clan A large group of people related to each other.

dye Powdered chemicals that can turn something a different color.

festival A celebration held every year.

garland A circle made of 3D decorations, such as flowers, that can be put around somebody's neck.

Mardi Gras A spring festival held in Catholic countries.

national dress An outfit associated with a country and sometimes worn on special occasions.

powwow A meeting event held by Native American people in the USA and Canada.

synagogue A Jewish temple.

traditional Something that has happened for a long time.

tribe A large group of related people who have the same leaders.

Further Information

Websites

National Geographic – Global Fashions
A photo gallery featuring portraits of clothing styles from around the world.
travel.nationalgeographic.com/travel/countries/global-fashion-photos/

The Kids Window
Written for kids by kids, this website talks about clothing styles from cultures around the world.
www.thekidswindow.co.uk/News/World_Clothing.htm

Talking Textiles
An interactive guide to clothing styles around the world, from both the past and the present.
www.childrensuniversity.manchester.ac.uk/interactives/art&design/talkingtextiles/costume/

Books

Adamson, Heather. *Clothes in Many Cultures.* North Mankato, MN: Capstone Press, 2009.

Ajmera, Maya. *What We Wear: Dressing Up Around the World.*

Lewis, Clare. *Clothes Around the World.* Portsmouth, NH: Heinemann Publishing, 2014.

Index